DESIGNING
Green
Communities

Design Thinking

for a Better World

Janice Dyer

CRABTREE
PUBLISHING COMPANY
WWW.CRABTREEBOOKS.COM

Author: Janice Dyer

Series research and development:
 Reagan Miller and Janine Deschenes

Editors: Janine Deschenes and Tracey Tanaka

Editorial director: Kathy Middleton

Editorial services: Clarity Content Services

Proofreader: Angela Kaelberer

**Production coordinator and prepress
 technician:** Samara Parent

Print coordinator: Katherine Berti

Cover design: Tammy McGarr

Design: David Montle

Photo Research: Linda Tanaka

Library and Archives Canada Cataloguing in Publication

Dyer, Janice, author
        Designing green communities / Janice Dyer.

(Design thinking for a better world)
Includes bibliographical references and index.
Issued in print and electronic formats.
ISBN 978-0-7787-4461-0 (hardcover).--
ISBN 978-0-7787-4540-2 (softcover).--
ISBN 978-1-4271-2036-6 (HTML)

        1. Community development--Environmental aspects--Juvenile literature. 2. Social participation--Environmental aspects--Juvenile literature. 3. Green movement--Juvenile literature. 4. Environmental responsibility--Juvenile literature. 5. Sustainable living--Juvenile literature. I. Title.

GE195.5.D94 2018   j363.7'0525   C2017-908090-3
                                                             C2017-908091-1

Library of Congress Cataloging-in-Publication Data

Names: Dyer, Janice, author.
Title: Designing green communities / Janice Dyer.
Description: New York : Crabtree Publishing Company, [2018] |
    Series: Design thinking for a better world |
    Includes bibliographical references and index.
Identifiers: LCCN 2017060081 (print) | LCCN 2018010918 (ebook) |
    ISBN 9781427120366 (Electronic) |
    ISBN 9780778744610 (hardcover) |
    ISBN 9780778745402 (pbk.)
Subjects: LCSH: Pollution prevention--Juvenile literature. | Social
    planning--Juvenile literature.
Classification: LCC TD176 (ebook) | LCC TD176 .D94 2018 (print) |
    DDC 363.73/6--dc23
LC record available at https://lccn.loc.gov/2017060081

Crabtree Publishing Company
www.crabtreebooks.com   1-800-387-7650

Printed in the U.S.A./052018/CG20180309

Published in Canada
Crabtree Publishing
616 Welland Ave.
St. Catharines, Ontario
L2M 5V6

Published in the United States
Crabtree Publishing
PMB 59051
350 Fifth Avenue, 59th Floor
New York, New York 10118

Published in the United Kingdom
Crabtree Publishing
Maritime House
Basin Road North, Hove
BN41 1WR

Published in Australia
Crabtree Publishing
3 Charles Street
Coburg North
VIC, 3058

Contents

What is Design Thinking?

Do you want to improve the world around you? Design thinking can help you to become a change maker!

Design thinking is a step-by-step process to solve real problems faced by real people. It starts with empathy. Empathy means understanding the feelings and perspectives of others. Empathy helps you focus on people's unique problems and develop solutions for them.

Green communities are environmentally friendly and have **green spaces**, or spaces with plants and trees. You can increase the amount of green space in your community by planting trees.

Focus on the User

The user is the person, group, or community who is facing a problem. A solution focused on the user is more likely to succeed. Design thinkers may fail on their first attempt to solve a user's problem—that's okay! Use what you learned to improve the next version of the design solution. This is called **failing forward**.

We are all responsible for protecting the global environment.

Where Did Design Thinking Come From?

Problem solvers have used design thinking for many years, though they called it different names. Today people of all ages and backgrounds use design thinking as a guide to becoming change makers in their communities.

Community Connections

Everyone is part of a community. A community is a place where people live, work, and play. A community can be small, like your neighborhood, or large, like your country or even the world! This book is about green communities, so you will learn how to use design thinking to come up with solutions that help communities be environmentally friendly.

Green community members "think globally" and "act locally." This means that they think about the health of the entire planet and take action in their own communities to fix environmental issues. People in green communities try to live in ways that minimize, or lessen, their impact on the environment. People in green communities improve and protect the environment closest to them. In turn, this helps protect the global environment that we all share.

Simon Jackson – Saving the Spirit Bear

Design Thinking in the Real World

Simon Jackson saw his first bear while camping at the age of 7. He learned that one type of bear, the spirit bear, was threatened with **extinction**. People hunted them for sport, and their habitat was being destroyed by activities such as **deforestation**. He studied the problem facing the bears and realized that they needed a habitat safe from hunting and logging.

When he was 13, Simon started the Spirit Bear Youth Coalition. He talked to students, politicians, and environmentalists to raise awareness about the problem that the spirit bears were facing. His campaign connected with more than six million people in 87 countries!

He asked people to protect the bears from hunting and habitat destruction. As a result of his work more than two-thirds of the spirit bear's habitat in British Columbia, Canada, is now protected.

The spirit bear is white, but isn't a polar bear! It is a black bear that has a rare **genetic** trait that makes it white instead of black.

The Design-Thinking Process

Design-Thinking Steps

The design-thinking process is a set of steps that guides problem solving. There are different versions of the process, but they all begin with empathy and put the user's needs first.

Observing or interacting with animals can help you develop empathy for them.

1. Empathize
Develop a deep understanding of the user's needs.

2. Define
Identify the user's point of view and define a problem to solve.

3. Ideate
Generate many creative ideas as possible solutions.

4. Prototype
Build a representation of the best idea.

5. Test
Share your prototype with the user and collect their feedback.

6. Reflect
Evaluate whether your solution met the user's need.

After completing all 6 steps, go back to the beginning and use what you learned to improve the next version of your prototype.

These steps are **iterative**, which means any of the steps can be repeated as you learn more about what works for the user. At each step, make improvements to your solution.

This book will guide you through the steps of the design-thinking process. We will review real-world case studies and introduce real change makers who are helping to protect the environment. Then you will design your own user-centered solutions to make your community greener.

Design thinking is a collaborative process. By working with others, you can approach a problem from many different perspectives.

Mindset Tips

Listen up	Remember that the user has a story to tell, so listen closely.
Dig deeper	If you don't understand something, ask questions.
Take turns	Let everyone have a chance to voice ideas and ask questions.
Get distracted	Creative ideas often come when you least expect, such as on a walk, during a game, or when you're daydreaming.
Be brave	Don't let shyness prevent you from contributing your ideas.

Empathize

What Is Empathy?

Empathy is the ability to understand the feelings and perspectives of others. To do this, you need to gather information about someone's feelings, beliefs, values, experiences, viewpoints, and needs. Empathy is sometimes called "need finding." A need is any requirement—physical, cultural, or social—that a person or group has.

What is an example of a need related to green communities? In order to survive, hawks need mature trees and open fields. Hawks help **urban** environments by eating rodents. Often as cities expand, trees are cut down and open fields become neighborhoods. A design thinker might do research to learn about the hawks' needs and the problems they face. The design thinker might identify that hawks need a safe habitat and work to preserve the hawk habitats in their community.

Hawks depend on trees and fields to hunt for food.

Why Is Empathy Important?

Empathy is important because it helps you focus on finding solutions that meet the specific needs of your user. Empathy helps the design thinker to see the problem from the user's point of view. The best solutions result from truly understanding the user's perspective.

Sometimes users have a problem but aren't able to think of a solution. Other times, people know the solution they need, but they aren't being heard by the people who create the solutions. In either case, empathy helps you identify their needs.

How to Empathize

Develop empathy for your users by learning about them. *Immerse* yourself in their lives, *engage* with them, and *observe* their lives in action. For example, Sean could spend time with fishers on their boats to see how they work with fishing line, and ask them questions about the challenge they face. He could read or watch information about risks to marine animals or volunteer at a rescue organization that helps marine animals injured by fishing line.

You can use more than just words to learn about your user. You or the user can make drawings, take photos, record quotes, tell stories, draw maps and other images, and visit special locations in the community.

These nets were abandoned and now present a risk to birds and animals.

Sean Russell – The Stow It-Don't Throw It Project

Empathy in the Real World

When Sean Russell was 16 years old, he worked at a marine laboratory near his home in Florida. He saw how dolphins and other ocean wildlife were hurt when people throw their fishing line into the ocean. As a result of his empathy for marine wildlife, Sean started the Stow It-Don't Throw It project.

Sean Russell works to prevent marine mammal injury by fishing line.

This dolphin was caught in fishing line and has almost lost its tail.

Sean learned that fishing line takes up to 600 years to decompose and that individual fishers had no way to dispose of it on their boats. As a result, fishers were throwing the nets into the ocean, instead of bringing them to shore for disposal. To help solve this problem, he designed a fishing line recycling bin out of recycled tennis ball containers so fishers could safely get rid of fishing line. Through this program, Sean inspires youth to give out fishing line recycling bins and start their own marine conservation projects.

Sean's empathy for the marine environment and for fishers led him to create a unique solution that addressed a problem in his community.

Sean Russell's innovative solution

Define

This stage is about identifying a specific user's need. To do this, you need to review what you learned during the empathy stage.

To help understand the problem being faced by dolphins and fishers in his community, Sean might have asked himself questions such as:

- What did I learn about dolphins and fishers?
- What needs stood out and why?
- How are the needs of the dolphins and fishers similar and different?
- Did the fishers suggest solutions?

Remember, this stage is not about finding solutions. It is about identifying a user's need, and a problem to solve. This is the beginning of your action plan!

Look for patterns, themes, and big ideas in the information you gathered during the empathy stage. Use a tool, like a 2 × 2 matrix, to help you organize your information.

To create his solution, Sean needed to learn about the dolphins' needs. Dolphins depend on clean ocean water with plentiful fish.

2 x 2 Matrix

A 2 × 2 matrix can help you identify the relationship between things:

- Draw a 2 × 2 matrix.
- Choose two categories and put opposites on either end (e.g., high impact and low impact, hard and easy).
- Sort your ideas by placing them on the matrix.
- Fill in the cells with the information you gathered.
- Answer questions such as: Which cells are fuller? Which are emptier? What patterns or themes stand out?

2 × 2 matrix		
HIGH Environmental Impact		
HARD for fishers	• Dispose of nets on land	• Dolphins killed or injured • Throw nets into the ocean	**EASY** for fishers
	• Store nets on board • Recycle nets on land • Repair nets	• Use a container to hold the nets until they can be repaired or recycled	
LOW Environmental Impact		

Define a Point of View

After you analyze the information learned at the empathy stage, write a point-of-view (POV) statement. A useful POV statement identifies the user's specific need, and the problem to be solved.

Good POV statements and questions should:

- Identify the user's need, and the problem that you will try to solve.
- Inspire you or your team
- Encourage you to create one solution for one user's need.

A small dolphin swims next to the left net of this shrimping boat off Biloxi and Ocean Springs Coast, USA.

TIPS:
Getting Started

Think back to Sean Russell's solution. To help create a POV statement, Sean might have asked himself:

- Who is the user?
- What needs does the user have?
- Why does this problem exist?

After learning more about the impacts of fishing line on dolphins, Sean might have written the following POV statement: "Dolphins are being injured by fishing line that is thrown into the ocean."

After Sean defined the dolphins and fishers as his users and their shared need of a safe way to dispose of fishing line, he might have created a point-of-view question. This helps design thinkers define the problem they will solve. Sean might have asked, "How can we develop a way to dispose of fishing line so that fishers don't throw it into the ocean?" Try these sentence starters to help you construct your POV question.

- How can we prevent…?
- How can we help…?
- How can we create a way to…?

Ideate

What Is Ideation?

Ideation means forming ideas. Now it's time to think about ways to address the needs of the users you identified in the define stage. In this stage, you are trying to answer your POV question. This can be fun because you get to use your imagination to create as many different solutions as possible.

Solution ideas can be a product, such as a tool or a website, or a process, such as a different way of doing things. For example, in the Stow It-Don't Throw It project, Sean developed both a tool and a process to address the injury and death of dolphins due to improper disposal of fishing line. Fishers started using a recycled tennis ball container (tool) to hold used fishing line until it could be brought to land for proper disposal (process).

It's All About Brainstorming

At this stage there are no bad ideas! Brainstorming is a way of generating lots of ideas quickly, whether big or small, practical or out-there. Pay attention to different perspectives and consider all possible solutions. Keep track of every idea. What might seem silly at first might lead to the best possible solution.

- Work as a team. Having more people can lead to more ideas. Be sure to record them, too—have at least one person take notes as the group brainstorms.
- Set a time limit. Take long enough for everyone to contribute, but remember you have more work to do.

Keep an eye on the time! Since this stage is so open-ended, it can be helpful to set a time limit so you stay on task.

Brainstorming Tools

- whiteboards and dry erase markers
- chalkboard and chalk
- poster paper and markers
- sticky notes, scrap paper, index cards, notebooks, and pens or pencils

TIPS: Pick an Idea

Now choose the best idea to move forward. Here are some ways to do this:

- **Blind voting** – Each person writes their favorite idea on a slip of paper. Sort the slips of paper to find out which idea got the most votes.

> Write your ideas on a piece of paper and then review all of them as a group

- **Sticky notes or dot voting** – List the ideas on a whiteboard, chalkboard or poster paper, and then have each person put a sticker beside their favorite ideas.

> Put ideas up on a wall or board. Then group ideas by topic or rank them.

Prototype

What Is a Prototype?

A prototype is a **model** or version of the idea you chose in the ideate step. When you create a prototype for the users to test, you are able to learn how the users will interact with the idea, what works, and what needs improving.

Create a prototype of your best solution idea. If your solution is a product, you might use everyday materials to build a prototype version of it. If your solution is a process, you might create a **storyboard** or video or use another method to explain how the process works. Keep in mind that your prototype should be simple and easy to create. You want to be able to easily make changes to your idea for the next version.

Use the supplies you have to create a model, or prototype of your idea.

Building a Prototype

Prototypes are anything the user can experience or interact with:

- Physical objects, such as a tool or model
  - Use paper, craft supplies, or found objects to create the object you want to test.

- A process, or different way of doing something
  - Use a storyboard, a diagram, images, sketches, or flow charts to show what the process will look like.

- A role-playing skit or scenario
  - Write or improvise a scene in which you, or someone else, act like the user and try out the prototype. Take notes while observing others work through the scenario.

- A computer website, program, or display
  - Use your computer skills to create or display a solution, or draw out your website and all of its parts on paper or a large board.

You could use your artistic skills to draw a picture showing your solution.

TIPS:
Getting Started

- Try not to spend too much time planning the perfect prototype. Remember you can revise and improve as you go.

- Remember your POV statement—stay focused on the users and their need.

- Remember your POV question—make sure that your prototype is a solution to the problem you are trying to solve.

Test

Putting it to the Test

To test your idea, let the user try your prototype and see if it solves the problem. Testing will reveal the strengths and weaknesses of your idea. This stage is about getting feedback from your users and learning what works and what doesn't.

The User's Experience

- Whenever possible, show, don't tell—explain your concept and then let the user try the prototype.

- Create an experience for the user that allows them to interact with your object, product, or presentation.

After your prototype is built, let your user or peers test it and give you feedback.

- If the user is not available to try the prototype, have classmates, peers, or others test it. Make sure you tell them what you learned about the user in the empathy stage before you have them "step into the user's shoes." Tell them your POV statement and question.

Getting Feedback

Watch the user (or tester) interact with your solution. Take notes or get permission to make recordings. Get feedback by asking questions starting with "why," "how," and "what":

- What worked, and why did it work?

- What did not work, and why?

- How can we improve the outcome?

Consider using a **survey** to collect as much feedback as possible.

If your prototype doesn't work as you expected, use what you learned to build a better solution. Remember, it is okay to fail forward.

A survey can help direct the questions you ask to collect feedback. It can also help you organize the feedback you gathered.

Reflecting on Results

Although the final step is dedicated to reflecting, keep in mind that reflection is part of each stage in the design-thinking process. With each step, think about your work and make improvements as needed.

Decide if the prototype met the needs of your user or how it could be improved.

Review the results of your prototype test.

How Do You Reflect?

Review your original POV statement and question. Review the feedback that you collected during the test step and analyze the results. You might use a tool, such as a 2 × 2 matrix or color-coded sticky notes, to organize the feedback you received.

Use the tool to answer the following questions:
- How well did the prototype meet the needs of the user?
- How can you improve the prototype to achieve better results?
- What might be the next iteration of the process?

Document and Present Your Results

Share your findings with others! You might write a short summary of the experience to document the design-thinking process and your results. A summary would describe each step and include your observations and the feedback of your users. Present the tools you used and highlight how the information you gathered illustrates your conclusions. Then make recommendations for the next iteration of the prototype.

Other ways to document your results are to write a journal entry, make a slide show, illustrate a story or drawing, create a video, or write or perform a song or poem.

After reflecting on your test results, compile your findings into a report.

PROJECT

Increasing Pollution

This symbol and note on sewer grates reminds people not to throw waste onto the street where it will be washed into the sewer system and eventually pollute local waterways.

What Is the Issue?

Pollution is anything that has harmful effects on the environment. When the air, water, and land are polluted, they become **contaminated**. This makes many natural resources dangerous for the living things that depend on them.

Air pollution causes serious health problems and contributes to **climate change** and **greenhouse gases**. Greenhouse gases are a form of air pollution that causes **global warming**. As a result of global warming, polar ice is melting, and the sea level is rising.

Sources of land and water pollution include oil spills, **pesticides**, **sewage**, and **solid waste**. Oil spills happen when pipelines or vessels carrying oil malfunction or have an accident, releasing the oil into water or on land. People use pesticides to kill insects that harm plants; however, they also harm the soil and helpful insects. Sewage, which is created by individuals and businesses, includes bathroom waste and industrial by-products such as dirty water and waste chemicals. Solid waste is the things that people throw away, such as furniture, electronics, and household garbage.

This garbage is polluting the water, but it is from land-based sources. This means that people threw the garbage into the street, rivers, or beaches, or that it came from a garbage dump or industrial area. This kind of garbage is carried to the ocean by storm drains, by floating downstream, or by the wind.

When levels of pollution increase, many different groups or **stakeholders** are affected. Some stakeholders that are affected by different types of pollution are:

- Marine life is affected by solid waste in the water, a type of marine pollution. Animals become entangled in **marine debris** such as fishing line, preventing them from eating, breathing, or swimming. Some birds, fish, and mammals die from eating debris, mistaking it for food.
- Plants and wildlife such as birds, mammals, shellfish, and fish may become sick or die when oil spills happen. Oil is **toxic**, so animals that ingest oil when they try to clean themselves can get sick or die.
- Communities that rely on fish are affected because they catch less fish than they did in the past. Global warming is leading to more floods, more droughts, rising water levels, and changes in water temperatures. These changes harm the populations of some types of fish.

Meet a
CHANGE MAKER

Leroy Mwasaru: The Human Waste Bioreactor

Leroy Mwasaru is a change maker in Kenya who created the Human Waste **Bioreactor**. His community had no clean water because sewage was leaking into the local river. He wondered how he could prevent sewage from contaminating the water source. Leroy brainstormed ideas with his peers at school and decided to try to find a way to use human waste as a sustainable, or renewable, source of fuel. That way, the waste was not being flushed as sewage and could be used for a new purpose as a clean source of energy in the community. Leroy built a prototype bioreactor that used animal and food waste for cooking. After testing this prototype, his next iteration was to use human waste, which was also successful. As a result of Leroy's Human Waste Bioreactor, sewage is no longer contaminating the local river, so the community has clean water and a renewable source of energy.

Many people in Leroy's community cook in their homes using the bioreactor technology.

Many communities have public latrines, or toilets, which may leach waste into local water sources.

Next, Leroy incorporated his project into a company called *Greenpact* that helps local communities access clean gas for cooking. Leroy also started *CampBuni** to give back to his community. It is a non-profit high school where kids in Kenya can learn Human-Centered Design Thinking and Entrepreneurship.

**Buni*—Swahili for Innovate

Leroy Mwasaru designed the Human Waste Bioreactor.

CASE

Effects of Marine Debris on Leatherback Sea Turtles

Marine pollution impacts many species, such as the leatherback sea turtle, which is considered endangered world-wide and is already extinct in Malaysia. Leatherback sea turtles are deep-diving sea turtles that live in the Pacific, Atlantic, and Indian oceans. They migrate long distances to tropical islands to nest and lay eggs. These turtles feed mostly on jellyfish.

In the Pacific Ocean, many leatherback sea turtles die each year because of plastic bags, which are a large portion of the garbage that floats in the ocean.

When the bags float through the water, they look like jellyfish. Thinking they are food, the turtles chase the bags and eat them. The turtles often become tangled in the bags and drown. When they eat the bags, the turtles eventually die because the bags clog up their insides and have no nutritional value.

The leatherback turtle returns to shore to lay eggs, then goes back to the deep ocean waters. While on shore, she and her eggs are at risk from hunters.

Leatherback sea turtles are not alone. Many ocean creatures, including seabirds, sea lions, and other turtle species struggle to survive the impacts of marine debris from land-based garbage.

- More than 7 million tons (6.35 metric tons) of garbage is dumped in oceans every year.
- More than 1 million seabirds die each year from ocean pollution.
- Americans dispose of more than 380 billion plastic bags and wraps each year.

This hawksbill turtle died because it could not escape marine pollution.

Empathy What challenges do leatherback sea turtles face because of plastic-bag pollution in the Pacific Ocean?

Define POV After you have used empathy to understand the plight of the leatherback sea turtles, create a POV statement defining their needs. Create a POV question that helps you start to solve their problem.

POV QUESTION PROMPT: **How can we prevent … ?**

CASE

Treating Birds Impacted by Oil Spills

Shawn works with an animal conservation and rescue organization in his community of Sausalito, California. Volunteers clean birds and look after them when they have been affected by oil spills. They need to wash the oil off the birds, rinse them, dry them, monitor them to make sure they are healthy enough to be released, and then release the healthy birds back into their habitat. This process takes a lot of time and can be costly, especially if the birds need extra medical attention after being cleaned.

The number of oil spills is increasing. More oil is being **extracted** from and shipped across the ocean, in addition to being drilled on land and shipped using trucks, trains, and pipelines. Shawn is part of a small team at the organization and is often overwhelmed by the number of birds that need help. He worries that there won't be enough money for the supplies they need to help the birds. He is also concerned that there won't be enough people available to help clean and care for the birds.

This bird is coated in oil from a spill. When the bird cleans its feathers, it will eat the oil and die.

Animal conservation workers clean oiled birds using gentle soap to break down the oil. Then they rinse the birds carefully. This process takes a long time since all the feathers have to be cleaned, and they may have to wash the bird several times to remove the oil.

Shawn is not alone. Many people around the world work to rescue injured marine animals after oil spills.

- In 2010, the BP Deepwater Horizon oil rig exploded, causing the worst oil spill in history with 210 million gallons (795 million liters) of oil spilling into the ocean.

- In the first three months after the BP Deepwater Horizon oil rig spill, conservation workers collected over 1,000 oiled birds from the Gulf Coast. More than half of them were already dead.

- An oiled bird will spend an average of two weeks in recovery after it is rescued.

The Design-Thinking Process

Empathy What factors are affecting Shawn's ability to do his job? How does it make him feel?

Define POV After you have used empathy to understand Shawn's point of view, create a POV statement defining his needs. Create a POV question that helps you to start to solve his problem.

POV QUESTION PROMPT: **How can we make it possible for … ?**

CASE

Effects of Climate Change on Family Fisheries

For generations, Franki's family has been fishing for Atlantic cod in the Gulf of Maine, off the East Coast of the United States. She has always been able to support her family as a fisher, but in recent years, she has caught fewer and fewer fish. She learned that climate change and global warming is increasing the temperature of shoreline waters.

The cod aren't **reproducing** successfully in the warm, shallow water, and the fish are following the colder water out to sea. Franki's boat is not big enough for her to fish safely in the deeper water, and she can't afford a new bigger boat.

She had hoped to pass the boat down to her children, but she doesn't know how much longer fishing can support her family. Sometimes she thinks about selling her boat and using the money to move her family to a town where she could train for a different job.

Atlantic cod can live more than 20 years and grow to over 75 pounds. There used to be lots of cod, but now it is in decline because of climate change and overfishing.

Fishing for Atlantic cod has been the livelihood for families in Canada and the United States for many generations.

Franki is not alone. Many fishers are struggling to support their families on declining fish numbers.

- 845 million people who rely on the fishing industry will be affected in the coming decades if fish populations continue to decline because of climate change.
- One billion people, mostly from **developing countries**, rely on fish for food.
- In 1991, Maine's Atlantic cod catch was 21 million pounds (9.5 million kilograms), but in 2016 it was down to less than 170,000 pounds (77,110 kg).

The Design-Thinking Process

Empathy How is Franki being affected by climate change? How does it make her feel?

Define POV After you have used empathy to understand Franki's point of view, create a POV statement defining her needs. Create a POV question that helps you start to solve her problem.

POV QUESTION PROMPT: **How can we support … ?**

Reducing Pollution

How might we lessen pollution in our communities?

Now it's your turn to make a difference! You will work through the design-thinking process to create a solution to lessen the impact of pollution for a person, a species, or a community.

Start by thinking about the three users facing problems in this section:

1. Leatherback sea turtles are dying because they eat marine debris such as plastic bags, thinking they are jellyfish.

2. Shawn, an animal conservation and rescue worker, feels overwhelmed by the number of birds impacted by oil spills.

3. Franki, a cod fisher, worries about her livelihood because fish are less plentiful than they used to be.

These women are helping to clean up a beach after an oil spill.

Which user would you like to help? Choose either leatherback sea turtles, Shawn, or Franki and use the design-thinking steps to create a solution to their problem.

Empathize

Use empathy to learn more about the user's point of view:
- Review their stories, challenges, and frustrations.
- Ask questions about their needs.

Define

Create a POV statement defining the user and their needs. Then, create a POV question that helps you start to solve the problem. Use the POV prompt from the case study to help you.

Ideate

It's time to brainstorm! Draw, sketch, or write as many ideas as possible. Organize your ideas and select one for the next stage.

Prototype

Create a prototype of your idea. Keep it simple, inexpensive, and easy. Remember that your prototype should be something the user can experience.

Test

Show, don't tell — have your users or peers test your prototype and ask for feedback. Observe your user's experience with the prototype and take notes on what works and what doesn't work.

Reflect

Reflect on the results of your test.
- Has your prototype met the needs of the user?
- What can you change?

Reflect on the design-thinking process:
- What did you learn?
- What could you do differently?

Now, improve your prototype through another iteration of the process.
When you are happy with your solution, share it with your peers.

Impact of Non-Renewable Energy

The world's population uses energy sources for power and fuel. Fossil fuels such as natural gas, oil, and coal are cheap sources of energy. These types of fuels took hundreds of millions of years to form. They are called **non-renewable** because they will run out.

Non-renewable energy sources also have a large environmental impact. They create pollution, because they have to be burned to turn into energy. Since most fossil fuels exist beneath Earth's surface, accessing and transporting them requires a lot of digging and damages a lot of land. In contrast, **renewable energy** refers to sources of power and fuel that come from the sun, wind, rivers, and tides. This type of energy is considered almost endless. Renewable energy is also a cleaner source of energy. It has a minimal impact on the environment and does not produce a lot of pollution.

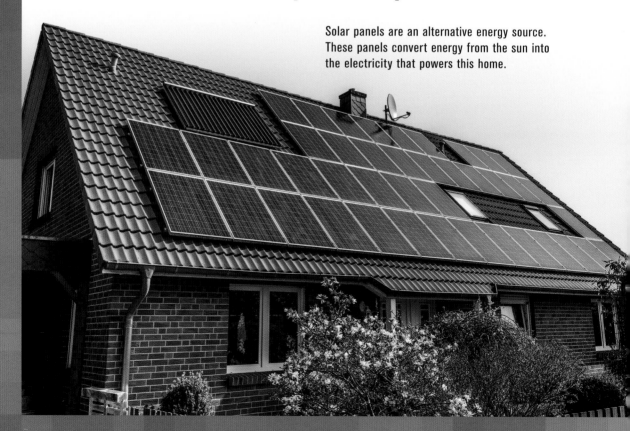

Solar panels are an alternative energy source. These panels convert energy from the sun into the electricity that powers this home.

When non-renewable energy is used, many different groups or stakeholders are affected. Here are some of the stakeholders affected by non-renewable energy use:

- Although working in coal mines and plants is a source of income for many people, those who work or live in coal industry communities are often negatively affected by the pollution created by mine sites and power plants. Toxins contaminate local air, soil, and water. Drinking local water, eating locally grown food, and breathing poor-quality air may lead to chronic health issues for wildlife, community members, and workers at the site.

- Plants, animals, and people are affected by the production of oil, a non-renewable energy source. **Oil sands** are one source of oil, where sand, clay, water, and thick oil are mixed together in nature. To get the oil out, the oil sands are dug up in large areas of land and then processed to separate and extract the oil. This process uses large amounts of water and energy. It also contaminates the local soil, water, plants, and wildlife.

- The construction of pipelines, which carry oil from place to place, can endanger animals and their habitats. Construction may destroy animal habitats or food sources. Animals may avoid the pipeline, resulting in conflicts and competition for resources with other animals in surrounding areas. Oil spills resulting from pipeline damage can contaminate soil and water.

Burning coal for power results in air pollution.

Sahil Doshi - Eco-Friendly Battery

Sahil Doshi, a 14-year-old student from Pittsburgh, Pennsylvania, learned that 1.2 billion people in developing countries don't have access to electricity because they live in poverty. He also learned that levels of air pollution in developing countries are increasing. Air pollution affects the health of communities. Sahil identified that the people living in these communities needed a cheap source of energy that wouldn't contribute to more air pollution. He designed an eco-friendly battery to meet their needs. The battery, called the PolluCell, changes carbon dioxide (an air pollutant) into electricity. Not only does it meet the need for clean, cheap electricity, but it takes the pollutant from the air to create the energy.

After winning several awards for his invention, Sahil Doshi presented his project at the White House Science Fair to then US President Barack Obama.

CASE

Effects of Burning Coal on Air Quality

Lin lives in a medium-sized town in China that has a coal mine and power plant nearby. Many people in her town, including her father and uncles, work in the coal industry to support their families. Her home and many others in her neighborhood have stoves and furnaces that burn coal for heat and cooking. As a result of all the coal burning, the town has very poor air quality.

Lin rides her bike to and from school each day. She always coughs during her ride and is often short of breath because the local air is so polluted. She usually wears a mask when she is outside, but the masks are uncomfortable and she wonders whether they

really work. Her mother always wore a mask outside, but now she has lung damage and can't work anymore. She is scared that her father will get sick too, because he inhales all the coal dust as well as the poor-quality air. She worries that she will have to quit school to help support her family if he gets sick. She wishes that there was a different way for her father to support the family.

These girls in China wear masks to protect them from air pollution.

Lin is not alone. Many communities suffer from poor air quality as a result of pollution from coal burning, but are dependent on the economic benefits of the coal industry.

- Coal burning is the single greatest source of air pollution in China, the United States, and Canada.
- Air pollution kills more than one million people in China each year.
- Coal is also burned to make steel, a type of metal. China's coal and steel sectors employ about 12 million people.

The Design-Thinking Process

Empathy How is Lin being affected by the coal industry in her community? How do the health challenges she faces make her feel?

Define POV After you have used empathy to understand Lin's point of view, create a POV statement defining her needs. Create a POV question that helps you start to solve her problem.

POV QUESTION PROMPT: **How can we help … ?**

CASE

Effects of Oil Sand Tailings Ponds on Migrating Ducks

Mallard ducks live in parts of Canada and the United States. Every year, when it gets cold, ducks migrate to warmer climates, then come back in the spring. During their migration, they look for bodies of water to land on so they can feed and rest.

In 2008, 1,606 ducks died after landing in one of the tailings ponds at an oil sands production site in northern Alberta, Canada. Tailings ponds are human-made bodies of waste water filled with pollutants created during the process of mining oil sands. The waste water is warm, so the ponds don't freeze over. When other ponds are frozen,

ducks land in the tailings ponds and many die from exposure to the contaminants. The ducks that survive to fly away may get sick and die later. This is because the contaminants are stuck to the ducks' feathers. If the feathers don't get clean, the duck can't stay warm, and when it tries to clean itself, it eats the oil and chemicals. Since ducks migrate to and from the oil sands area every year, many ducks will keep dying as they continue to land in the tailings ponds.

Ducks, such as mallards, depend on clean lakes, ponds, and ocean shorelines for their food and habitat.

Oil sands development impacts large amounts of land. Currently, the active mining footprint of this oil sands production area in Alberta, Canada, is about 187,800 acres (76,000 hectares), about the size of the city of Austin, Texas.

Mallard ducks and Canada are not the only species or country affected by tailings ponds.

- 43 different species of birds have died from tailings pond exposure at Canadian oil sands.
- Duck counts at one tailings pond recorded 2,700 ducks flying over in one day, and over 16,000 birds of various kinds were observed during the migration season.
- The United States also has oil sands production. It is located in Utah and covers 11,535 acres (4,688 hectares).

 ## The Design-Thinking Process

Empathy How are mallards being affected by oil sands production?

Define POV After you have used empathy to understand your user, create a POV statement to define the user and their needs. Create a POV question that helps you start to solve the problem.

POV QUESTION PROMPT: **How can we prevent … ?**

 CASE

The Dakota Access Pipeline and the Standing Rock Sioux Reservation

The residents of the Standing Rock Sioux **reservation** in North Dakota, USA, have protested the Dakota Access Pipeline since it was announced in 2014.

In the summer of 2016, Janet stayed with her family at the Sacred Stone Camp, which was created for people to gather, camp, and protest the pipeline.

Every day, she cooked at the camp with her mother while her aunt, uncle, and grandmother went to the construction site with their protest signs. Her mother told her that they were trying to stop the construction of an oil pipeline across the nearby Missouri River, because they were worried that if the oil from the pipeline spilled into the river, they would have no clean water to drink.

One day, the state troopers tried to evict them from the camp. It was really scary because she saw some people get hurt, and her aunt and uncle were arrested and dragged away. While they were in jail, her grandmother kept protesting. Janet asked her grandmother why she was still protesting when she might get hurt or arrested. She said that the river had always provided their people with clean water, and now it was their duty to protect it. The camp was closed in February 2017. The pipeline was completed in April 2017, and the first oil was delivered

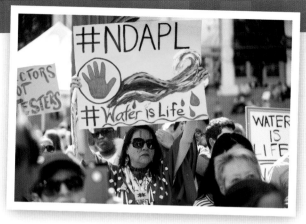

Protesters worry that the Dakota Access Pipeline will impact water quality.

through the pipeline May 2017.

Now that the pipeline construction is complete, Janet's family and other members of the Standing Rock Sioux reservation have ongoing concerns. The completed pipeline crosses the river only 10 miles (16 kilometers) upstream of their water system. They worry that a spill from the pipeline will pollute their only source of drinking water for generations.

People and ildlife are unable to use water and land if it becomes contaminated with oil leaking from a pipeline. The Standing Rock Sioux reservation is not the only community impacted by pipelines.

- There have been over 3,300 oil and gas pipeline leaks across the United States since 2010.
- In Canada, an average of 250 pipeline leaks occur each year.
- Thousands of people in Italy are protesting the Euro-Caspian Mega Pipeline, which will bring oil from Azerbaijan to Italy.

 ## The Design-Thinking Process

Empathy How are the people of the Standing Rock Sioux reservation affected by the Dakota Access Pipeline? What challenges does the pipeline create for them? How do they feel?

Define POV After you have used empathy to understand the point of view of the residents of the Standing Rock Sioux reservation, create a POV statement defining their needs. Create a POV question that helps you start to solve their problem.

POV QUESTION PROMPT: **How can we help … ?**

Promoting Renewable Energy

How can we promote the use of renewable, more sustainable energy?

Now it's your turn to make a difference! You will work through the design-thinking process to develop a solution to promote the use of renewable, sustainable energy for a person, a group, or a community.

Start by thinking about the three users facing problems in this section:

1. Lin's health, and that of her community, is being affected by coal burning.

2. Oil sands production is affecting the health of migratory birds such as mallard ducks.

3. The people of the Standing Rock Sioux reservation are concerned about oil spills from the Dakota Access Pipeline. They worry about their only water source becoming contaminated and what might happen to their community if there is no water to drink.

Many people have protested against the Dakota Access Pipeline. Protesting is a way to speak out against something. The Standing Rock protests drew a lot of public attention to the issue and created support for the community.

Which user would you like to help? Choose either Lin, mallard ducks, or the Standing Rock Sioux reservation and use the design-thinking steps to create a solution to their problem.

Empathize

Use empathy to learn more about the user's point of view.
- Ask questions about their needs.
- Watch videos and read articles.

Define

Create a POV statement defining the user and their needs. Then, create a POV question that helps you start to solve the problem. Use the POV prompt from the case study to help you.

Ideate

It's time to brainstorm! Draw, sketch, or write as many ideas as possible. Organize your ideas and select one for the next stage

Prototype

Create a prototype of your idea. Keep it simple and inexpensive. Remember that your prototype should be something the user can experience.

Test

Show, don't tell — have your users or peers test your prototype and ask for feedback. Observe your user's experience with the prototype and take notes on what works and what doesn't work.

Reflect

Reflect on the results of your test.
- Has your prototype met the needs of the user?
- What can you change?

Reflect on the design-thinking process:
- What did you learn?
- What could you do differently?

Now, improve your prototype through another iteration of the process.
When you are happy with your solution, share it with your peers.

Large Ecological Footprints

We all need food, water, shelter, and heat to survive. Earth's resources help meet these needs. Our ecological footprint is the amount of resources we use to meet our needs and the amount of waste we produce. It can also include the amount of land that we use to live on or energy we use to power our days.

If you walk to school or work, you have a smaller ecological footprint than someone who drives alone in a car, because the car uses fossil fuels and walking does not. The more resources you use, the larger your ecological footprint is. If we use too much of Earth's land and resources to meet our needs, Earth may not have enough resources for everyone to live. Urbanization, deforestation, and waste production contribute to the size of our ecological footprint, which affects many different groups or stakeholders.

Urbanization replaces green spaces such as forests and agricultural land with housing and business developments. The amount of land we use for housing is part of our ecological footprint. If that land had been used to grow food, or support wildlife, the ecological footprint is even bigger.

Green spaces can help reduce the negative impacts of urbanization. These spaces, such as parks, forests, and creeks provide habitat for local wildlife and allow people to connect with nature.

- Increasing urbanization can have a negative effect on plants, animals, and people. The replacement of green spaces with housing or business developments is part of the ecological footprint created by humans around the world.

- Many communities are negatively impacted by deforestation. As cities and farmland expand, forests are often cut down to make space. Deforestation is part of the global ecological footprint of humans. Forests provide homes for wildlife and capture greenhouse gases. They also help prevent landslides and flooding. The most dramatic effect of deforestation is the loss of wildlife habitat, causing species to become endangered.

- Many communities are running out of room in their landfills. As a result, some cities send their garbage to other cities that still have space. Transportation of garbage contributes to a larger ecological footprint. Experts warn that we have to reduce our waste production and recycle more, or we will have to continue to build more landfills and incinerators, or increase shipping of garbage to other communities that have room in their landfills.

Lynnea Shuck - Junior Refuge Ranger Program

Lynnea put herself in the shoes of young learners to design her program.

Lynnea Shuck is a high-school student from California, where many types of unique ecosystems are conserved by **National Wildlife Refuges**. Lynnea observed that children did not always have opportunities to learn about the exciting natural world around them and as a result, were not engaged in protecting the environment. She considered how she would have wanted to learn about the environment when she was younger. She was determined to find a way to encourage children to become involved in habitat and endangered species conservation. Lynnea designed the Junior Refuge Ranger Program, an educational program to encourage children to participate in the conservation of natural habitats and gain an appreciation for the National Wildlife Refuge System. Her goal is to give children experiences at National Wildlife Refuges in a hands-on and engaging way and encourage them to get involved in protecting the environment and living things in their communities. Her easy-to-use program has been implemented at other National Wildlife Refuges around the country, from California and Nevada to New York.

CASE

Effects of Urbanization on Birds

Quinten lives in Chicago, Illinois, and rides his bicycle to school every day. He watched a TV program about birds and city parks and decided to find a place he could bird-watch. There is no park in his neighborhood and no trees in his schoolyard, but a few miles away, he found a small field of grass with some trees and big plants. There were so many birds! He started to go every day after school to watch the birds. Quinten became so interested in birds that he did his class project on bird habitats. He learned that green spaces, such as parks, forests, and ponds, were all important habitats for birds.

One day, Quinten was shocked to see bulldozers and other equipment clearing the field for a new housing development. Since they started building, he never sees birds. He knows that when the trees and plants were cut down, the birds went away to find a new home.

He always felt happy when he sat quietly watching the birds. Now he has nowhere to go after school and is bored all the time. He wishes he could talk to someone about how to help the birds, but no one else seems to care.

Many cities have no green spaces. As a result, birds and other wildlife have nowhere to live.

The American Goldfinch lives in meadows and woodlands. They can live in cities if there are trees and green spaces.

Quinten is not alone in his concern for urban birds. Many people are working to improve bird habitat in cities.

- Researchers at Stanford University found that adding one tree to a pasture can increase the number of bird species seen from zero to 80.

- The North American Bird Conservation Initiative says that more than one-third of North American bird species are at risk of extinction.

- Scientists in New Jersey have found that only 8% of bird species are found in cities, compared to non-urban areas.

The Design-Thinking Process

Empathy What impact does urbanization have on Quinten? What kinds of challenges do birds experience as a result of urbanization?

Define POV After you have used empathy to understand Quinten's point of view, create a POV statement defining his need. Create a POV question that helps you start to solve his problem.

POV QUESTION PROMPT: **How can we encourage … ?**

 CASE

Deforestation and Habitat Loss

Maria's hometown in Brazil is close to the Amazon rainforest. Maria's family runs a small company that takes tourists into the forest and on the river to see local wildlife. She loves it when she gets to see the monkeys and likes to tell the tourists about them. Her favorite monkey is the Bald Uakari. From the family's riverboat, the monkeys can often be seen in large groups hanging out in the trees by the riverside.

As each year passes, Maria notices that they have to drive further and further to take the tourists out to forested areas. The land between her town and the forest has been cut down and burned to provide land for grazing cows and growing sugarcane. She knows that all the animals that used to live there are either dead or have gone further into the forest to find a new home. She sees fewer monkeys every time she goes out on the riverboat with a tour group.

It's getting harder to point out monkeys for the tourists to photograph. One of the tourists even got angry because he did not see any monkeys. Maria is worried about the Bald Uakari monkey and wonders how many other animals are disappearing because of deforestation. Her family is also afraid that their tourism business will suffer. They need it to survive.

Bald Uakari monkeys are bald, with bright-red faces and long, shaggy hair. They are threatened by deforestation in the Amazon.

39

In the Amazon, large amounts of forested land are cleared of trees and then burned to make room for cattle ranching and agriculture.

Maria is not alone. Many human and animal communities are negatively impacted by deforestation of the Amazon rainforest.

- More than 20% of the world's oxygen is produced by the trees and plants in the Amazon rainforest.
- 3.5 million acres (1.4 million hectares) of the Amazon rainforest are cut down every year.
- There are over 200 species of endangered animals in the Amazon rainforest, including the jaguar, the macaw, the three-toed sloth, and the Amazon river dolphin. One-third of the Bald Uakari monkey population has already died due to deforestation.

The Design-Thinking Process

Empathy What kinds of challenges does Maria face as a result of deforestation? How does this make her feel?

Define POV After you have used empathy to understand Maria's point of view, create a POV statement defining her needs. Create a POV question that helps you start to solve the problem.

POV QUESTION PROMPT: **How can we prevent ... ?**

CASE

Increasing Waste in Communities

Oliver lives in a medium-sized town that is running out of room in its landfill. To deal with the problem, the town is transporting its waste to other towns, but there are fewer towns willing to accept the trash.

At Oliver's school, they are trying to reduce their ecological footprint. They focus on putting paper and plastics from their lunches and study materials into the recycling bin instead of the garbage. Last year, the senior class tried a composting project, but it was smelly and messy, and they had nowhere to take the compost. The program was stopped, and now they just throw food waste in the garbage.

Everyone seems to be making an effort, but he heard from his older cousin, who works at the recycling depot, that lots of recycling bin contents end up going into the garbage because there is too much food waste on them. He also said that people often throw things such as electronics, batteries, and paint into the garbage, because they don't know how to recycle them, or don't want to drive to the depot, where they can safely dispose of toxic products.

Oliver wonders how he could improve the waste problem in his community.

Landfills are areas of land where waste is disposed.

Oliver's town is not alone. Communities across the United States and Canada struggle with waste disposal issues.

- The United States produces 30 percent of the world's waste.
- Electronic waste represents 70 percent of toxic waste in American landfills, but is only 2 percent of the waste discarded.
- It takes up to 500 years for a plastic bottle to decompose. Americans use 2.5 million plastic bottles per hour.

The Design-Thinking Process

Empathy What challenges do Oliver and his community face in trying to reduce the amount of waste they produce? How do these challenges affect them?

Define POV After you have used empathy to understand Oliver's point of view, create a POV statement defining his needs. Create a POV question that helps you start to solve his problem.

POV QUESTION PROMPT: **How might we help … ?**

Reducing Our Ecological Footprint

How can we reduce our ecological footprint?

Now it's your turn to make a difference! You will work through the design-thinking process to create a solution to help a person, group, or community reduce their ecological footprint.

Start by thinking about the three users facing problems in this section:

1. Quinten is concerned about the birds in his community. He feels sad and bored, because he can't bird-watch after school anymore. Urbanization is destroying the bird habitat in his community.

2. Deforestation is ruining the habitat for wildlife such as the Bald Uakari monkey in the Amazon rainforest near Maria's town in Brazil.

3. Oliver's community is running out of room for the garbage it produces. Oliver wants to help his community find ways to increase recycling and composting.

Composting is another important way to reduce the amount of waste that goes to landfills. Compost is made by mixing the remains of food and plants into soil and letting it decompose. The resulting material is very high in nutrients and can be used as fertilizer.

Which student would you like to help? Choose either Quinten, Maria, or Oliver and use the design-thinking steps to create a solution to their problem.

Empathize

Use empathy to learn more about the user's point of view.
- Listen to their stories, challenges, and frustrations.
- Ask questions about their needs.

Define

Create a POV statement defining the user and their needs. Then, create a POV question that helps you start to solve the problem. Use the POV prompt from the case study to help you.

Ideate

It's time to brainstorm! Draw, sketch, or write as many ideas as possible. Organize your ideas and select one for the next stage.

Prototype

Create a prototype of your idea. Keep it simple, inexpensive, and easy. Remember that your prototype should be something the user can experience.

Test

Show, don't tell — have your users or peers test your prototype and ask for feedback. Observe your user's experience with the prototype and take notes on what works and what doesn't work.

Reflect

Reflect on the results of your test.
- Has your prototype met the needs of the user?
- What can you change?

Reflect on the design-thinking process:
- What did you learn?
- What could you do differently?

Now, improve your prototype through another iteration of the process. When you are happy with your solution, share it with your peers.

What's Next for Design Thinking?

You are! Use design thinking to promote environmentally sustainable practices in your community. Look around your home, neighborhood, school, or city to identify users and their needs. Then, create a solution that addresses that need.

Students all over the world are helping solve environmental issues in their communities.

- Ana Humphrey from Virginia created a calculator to determine how much wetland is needed to keep waterways clean and prevent outbreaks of diseases carried in water.
- Ryan Hickman started Ryan's Recycling to collect and sort cans and bottles for customers and bring them to recycling centers to prevent them from reaching the ocean.
- Doorae Shin from Hawaii successfully created a petition to ban Styrofoam products on her school campus. She is now working to have these products banned in the state.
- Alejandro Abarcia of Chile designed a system to collect and store water from mist and dew on the slopes of hills and use the water for agriculture.

Design thinking can help you make a real difference in your community. You don't have to change the entire world—just your corner of it! Be a change maker!

Here are some ways to use design thinking to promote environmentally sustainable practices and make your community a green community:

- Join a group that is promoting green community projects. This may inspire you to develop a new solution to an ongoing problem.
- Do research to learn more about green community projects. How could you adapt these ideas for use in your own community?
- What environmental issue are you passionate about? How can you learn more about how the issue affects your community?

GREEN PROJECT

Learning More

Brower Youth Award
This award recognizes youth leaders who have made important contributions to the environmental movement. Visit the website to read about award winners and their projects.
http://www.broweryouthawards.org

Design Other 90 Network
This website features projects, proposals, and solutions that show how design can transform and save lives.
http://www.designother90.org

Ideo.com
This helpful websites offers articles about education, energy, and environmental issues.
https://www.ideo.com/work/education

Lundin Foundation
This foundation supports community growth in countries around the world. Visit this link to read about some of their solutions to environmental issues.
http://www.lundinfoundation.org/social-and-environmental-innovation/

NASA
This NASA site maintains and shares global climate change statistics and information.
https://climate.nasa.gov/

Practical Action
This organization addresses poverty in developing countries using technology and skills building.
https://practicalaction.org/design-for-a-better-world

The Marine Mammal Center
This is the primary hospital for seals and other marine animals that have been impacted by oil spills.
http://www.marinemammalcenter.org/what-we-do/rescue/oil-spill-response.html

Source Links

Introductory Material

"An Introduction to Design Thinking Process Guide." Institute of Design at Stanford. https://dschool-old.stanford.edu/sandbox/groups/designresources/wiki/36873/attachments/74b3d/ModeGuideBOOTCAMP2010L.pdf

Bains, Camille. "Simon Jackson, Spirit Bear Advocate, Named A Guardian Angel of the Planet." Huffpost/The Canadian Press. June 07, 2013. http://www.huffingtonpost.ca/2013/06/07/simon-jackson-guardian-angels-of-the-planet_n_3404424.html

Dam, Rikke, and Teo Siang. "Stage 2 in the Design Thinking Process: Define the Problem and Interpret the Results." Interaction Design Foundation. September 2017. https://www.interaction-design.org/literature/article/stage-2-inthe-design-thinking-process-define-the-problem-and-interpret-the-results

Drews, Christiane. "The Future of Innovation…Using Design Thinking Interdisciplinary." The Future of Innovation. 2009. http://thefutureofinnovation.org/contributions/view/671/the_future_of_innovation_using_design_thinking_interdisciplinary

"Everything you need to know about spirit bear holidays" Natural World Safaris. https://www.naturalworldsafaris.com/wildlife/spirit-bears

Mohamed, Farah. "Since 13, he's been fighting to protect B.C.'s spirit bear." *The Globe and Mail*. September 26, 2011. https://beta.theglobeandmail.com/life/giving/since-13-hes-been-fighting-to-protect-bcs-spirit-bear/article558627/?ref=http://www.theglobeandmail.com

"Redesigning how we learn." Henry Ford Learning Institute. https://hfli.org/redesigning-how-we-learn/

Shoumatoff, Alex. "This Rare, White Bear May Be the Key to Saving a Canadian Rainforest." Smithsonian.com. September 2015. https://www.smithsonianmag.com/science-nature/rare-white-bear-key-saving-canadian-rainforest-180956330/

Project: Increasing Pollution

"Atlantic Cod overview." NOAA Fisheries. https://www.fisheries.noaa.gov/species/atlantic-cod

Court, Alex. "Cooking with gas: Teenager brings poop power to Kenyan school." CNN. February 26, 2015. http://www.cnn.com/2015/02/26/business/poo-power-kenya/

Dell'Amore, Christine. "Oil-Coated Gulf Birds Better Off Dead?" National Geographic News. June 10, 2010. https://news.nationalgeographic.com/news/2010/06/100608-gulf-oil-spill-birds-science-environment/

"Effects of Global Warming." National Geographic. http://www.nationalgeographic.com/environment/global-warming/global-warming-effects/

Jackson, Stephen T. "Climate change." Encyclopedia Britannica. https://www.britannica.com/science/climate-change

Lavell, Marianne. "Collapse of New England's iconic cod tied to climate change." *Science Magazine*. October 29, 2015. http://www.sciencemag.org/news/2015/10/collapse-new-england-s-iconic-cod-tied-climate-change

Mann, Michael, and Henrik Selin. "Global warming." Encyclopedia Britannica. https://www.britannica.com/science/global-warming

"Marine Debris." Beachapedia. http://www.beachapedia.org/Marine_Debris

Source Links

"Oil Tanker Spill Statistics 2017." ITOPF. http://www.itopf.com/knowledge-resources/data-statistics/statistics/

"Leatherback Sea Turtles." See Turtles Org. www.seeturtles.org/ocena-plastic, http://www.seeturtles.org/leatherback-turtles

"Sean Russell, Stow It-Don't Throw It." The Pollination Project. 2015. https://thepollinationproject.org/grants-awarded/sean-russell-stow-it-dont-throw-it

"The Problem with Marine Debris." State Water Resources Control Board, Division of Water Quality. https://www.waterboards.ca.gov/water_issues/programs/swamp/docs/cwt/guidance/4312.pdf

"What is pollution?" Conserve Energy Future. http://www.conserve-energy-future.com/pollutiontypes.php

Project: Non-renewable Energy

"Harmful effects of non-renewable resources on the environment." Greentumble. February 23, 2017. http://greentumble.com/harmful-effects-of-non-renewable-resources-on-the-environment/

"Indian-American boy is America's Top Young Scientist." The Indian Diaspora. October 28, 2014. http://www.india.com/theindian-diaspora/indian-american-boy-is-americas-topyoung-scientist-182209/

"Land Usage - Environment." *Oil Sands Magazine*. http://www.oilsandsmagazine.com/technical/environment/land-usage

"Non-renewable energy." National Geographic. https://www.nationalgeographic.org/encyclopedia/non-renewable-energy/

Savedge, Jenn. "9 young inventors who may just save the world." Mother Nature Network. October 20, 2014. https://www.mnn.com/green-tech/research-innovations/blogs/9-young-inventors-who-may-just-save-the-world

Selin, Noelle Eckley. "Renewable energy." Encyclopedia Britannica. https://www.britannica.com/science/renewable-energy. Accessed 2018.

"The Environmental Impact of the Oil Sands: A Research Project for Secondary School Science Students." SFU Center for Education, Law, and Society. 2011. http://www.sfu.ca/sfublogs-archive/research/cels/uploads/2012/11/environmental-impact-of-the-oil-sands.pdf

Worland, Justin. "What to Know About the Dakota Access Pipeline Protests." Time. October 28, 2016. http://time.com/4548566/dakota-access-pipeline-standing-rock-sioux/

Yao, Kevin, and Meng Meng. "China expects to lay off 1.8 million workers in coal, steel sectors." Reuters. February 28, 2016. https://www.reuters.com/article/us-china-economy-employment/china-expects-to-lay-off-1-8-million-workers-in-coal-steel-sectors-idUSKCN0W205X

Project: Large Ecological Footprints

"37 ways to reduce trash in your home." Small Footprint Family. https://www.smallfootprintfamily.com/37-ways-to-reduce-trash

"Believe It! These Red-Faced Primates Known as Uakari Actually Exist for Real." Unbelievable Facts. May 11, 2016. https://www.unbelievable-facts.com/2016/05/uakari-red-faced-primates.html

Chrobak, Ula. "Even 1 tree adds biodiversity to in-between areas." Stanford University. October 25, 2016. http://www.futurity.org/trees-biodiversity-1280382-2/

"Closed Loop Plastics." Startup Compete. January 31, 2017. http://startupcompete.co/startup-idea/consumer-goods-green-materials/closed-loop-plastics/58414

Cordell, Doug. "Lynnea Shuck Honored by Earth Island Institute for Creating Refuge's Junior Ranger Program." San Francisco Bay Wildlife Society. http://sfbws.com/blog/2014/09/29/lynnea-shuck-honored-earth-island-institute-creating-refuge%E2%80%99s-junior-ranger-program

"Ecological footprint." Sustainable Measures. http://www.sustainablemeasures.com/node/102

Epstein, Paul. "Young South Bay habitat hero engages kids in refuge conservation." Bay Nature. November 20, 2014. https://baynature.org/article/south-bay-habitat-hero-engages- youth-conservation/

Healthy Parks Healthy People Central. Urban planning and the importance of green space in cities to human and environmental health. http://www.hphpcentral.com/article/urban-planning-and-the-importance-of-green-space-in-cities-to-human-and-environmental-health. Accessed 2018.

"Conservation Plants for Birds." National Audubon Society. http://tx.audubon.org/conservation/plants-birds

"Planting native species to help birds." Bird Life International - Americas. December 12, 2016. http://www.birdlife.org/americas/news/planting-native-species-help-birds

"Threats: Deforestation." World Wildlife Federation (WWF). https://www.worldwildlife.org/threats/deforestation

"Top tips to improve urban bird diversity." European Commission DG ENV. News Alert Issue 256. October 6, 2011. http://ec.europa.eu/environment/integration/research/newsalert/pdf/256na7_en.pdf

"Trash Troubles: Ontario's garbage continues to outstrip available landfill space." Durham Region.com reprinted from Oshawa This Week. October 19, 2011. https://www.durhamregion.com/community-story/3499160-trash-troubles-ontario-s-garbage-continues-to-outstrip-available-landfill-space/

"Urban green spaces." World Health Organization. http://www.who.int/sustainable-development/cities/health-risks/urban-green-space/en/

WWF Global. Ecological Footprint. http://wwf.panda.org/about_our_earth/teacher_resources/webfieldtrips/ecological_balance/eco_footprint/

Glossary

bioreactor A piece of equipment in which a biological process or reaction takes place

climate change Modification of Earth's climate, or usual weather, as a result of changes in the atmosphere

contaminate To make something, such as a resource, unclean or not pure

deforestation Clearing a wide area of trees

developing countries Countries that have a poor, or less developed, economy

extinction The death of a species

extracted Something that is taken out of its original location

failing forward When design thinkers use their mistakes or failures to improve on their next try

genetic A feature of heredity, or inherited from our ancestors

global warming Increase in long-term average air temperatures at Earth's surface

green communities Communities that do as much as they can to help protect the environment

green spaces Areas of grass, trees, or other vegetation in an urban environment

greenhouse gases A gas that contributes to global warming

iterative When something is done repeatedly, usually in a slightly different way

marine debris Items of garbage that have been disposed of in the ocean

model A small copy of something that lets us know what it looks like

National Wildlife Refuges A place where animals are protected

non-renewable energy Comes from energy sources that will run out or will not be replenished for thousands/millions of years; fossil fuels include coal, petroleum (oil), and natural gas

oil sands Sand, clay, water, and thick oil that are mixed together in nature.

pesticides Substances used to destroy insects that harm plants or animals

pollution Something that has harmful effects on the environment

prototype The first model of something

renewable energy Comes from replenishable sources such as the Sun, wind, and tides

reproducing The act by which offspring are produced by their biological parents

reservation In the United States, federal Indian reservations are areas of land reserved for and governed by tribes of Native Americans. In Canada, reserves are land set aside for and governed by First Nations peoples.

sewage Waste water and matter usually carried by sewers

solid waste Any unwanted product that is not a liquid or gas

stakeholder The person who is experiencing a problem and will be using the solution

storyboard A set of drawings that outline a scenario

survey collecting answers to a list of questions from many people

toxic Poisonous

urban Related to a city

urbanization The process by which an area becomes more city-like, with towns and cities forming and growing larger

Index

About the Author

Janice Dyer has been working as a freelance editor and writer for over 20 years. She has written several nonfiction books for kids. She edits textbooks and other educational materials, nonfiction books, and reports.